THOUGHTS AND FEELINGS

VOLUME ONE

DANIEL CHIDIAC

UNDERCOVER

PUBLISHING HOUSE

First published by Undercover Publishing House.

ISBN: 978-0-9871665-2-4

Note from the author...

"I often have these deep thoughts and feelings that I express in the only way I know how...through words. I don't usually share them as most are a passing moment, a sudden reflection or a personal perspective of my experiences. But now, I really feel it's time to release them for others to enjoy, connect with or to gain inspiration from. I invite you to get a pencil, co-write and express yourself in the same way within this book. You may write something in relation to what I have written or something completely different...that side of the book is yours. And in the end, you will have your own Thoughts and Feelings Volume One book written. If you do not feel ready to write anything, that is also fine. I hope you enjoy the read."

Love,
Daniel Chidiac

THOUGHTS AND FEELINGS

VOLUME ONE

Only when you compare yourself with others, do you feel like you've wasted time. When you focus on your own experiences, what you've gone through and what you've learnt, you realise you're right on time.

When you realise you never really loved them for who they were, you get over it quicker. You're more upset with yourself for making-out that you loved them, when you really just wanted them to love you.

Often times, because we have been hurt after opening-up, we close-off and hurt others. If you've been hurt, try to treat others with respect and kindness, even if you're still not ready to open-up again…they might be the ones that are opening for you, just like you were for that last person.

When someone is rude and arrogant, they are insecure. They aren't happy. True confidence makes you respectful and polite. It's a higher energy, a higher vibration. When I meet someone who is rude or arrogant, I ask them, "Is everything ok?"

The Universal energy that is used to attract does not respond well to you always being anxious over what you want. Being at peace with what you've got now doesn't mean that's all you will ever get. That's actually the energy you need to attract what you want.

The Universe doesn't reward that anxious energy because it knows you will never be at peace no matter what you get. It wants to create enlightened beings... not distant itself from that. First find peace with what you have, then pursue what you want. Ever notice things manifest when you're at peace, living your life and least expecting them? Work, but work with the freedom of knowing you already have everything you need.

I should be content anywhere, because the only thing that truly makes me content is love and light. And they are always inside me, no matter where my life takes me. That's what gives me warmth and comfort.

Not every rejection is a reflection of your femininity or masculinity. Some people have very deep issues of their own, and their rejection or mistreatment of you often has nothing to do with you at all.

I don't know if loving someone is negative or positive. I don't know if it gives to us or takes from us. Maybe it's both, equally. But isn't life about balance?

Have you ever noticed that often times when you get heartbroken or feel rejection on a level that shakes your whole world, you were in a really good place before then? And then you say to your friends, "I don't know how this happened. Before I met this person I was in such a great place...it came out of nowhere."

There's this misconception that we get attached to people when we are feeling down or in a low state of being, but that's not always the case. Often times when we are on a high, we are at our most vulnerable. It's when our guard is fully down. And that's because we have forgotten to stay vigilant, remember our experiences and stay self-aware. Whatever stage you're in, always, always, stay aware.

I subconsciously used to go in trusting every word they said. I don't do that anymore. I've had enough experience to know that very rarely works. And some say, "But, you need to be open." The thing is, I am now...truly open. Open to them not being who they are telling me they are when we first meet. It's not like I go into something negatively or expecting the worst, but I stay vigilant. I don't know who you are or what you want from me yet. To me, trust is built, it's earned...not just given. Time tells all.

If you're sitting there constantly dwelling over things you wish you had've done differently - all the times you've gone back to the same kinds of people, all the mistakes you've made, all the times you've repeated the same habits you swore you wouldn't again, I have a message for you…I've been there. The only reason you're beating yourself up so much is because you have forgotten that change takes time and that life is a journey. Be patient with yourself, true change takes time. And sometimes…many, many, of the same experiences.

One thing I'm learning as I get older...don't be so emotionally attached to the outcome. It's giving me a freedom I've never felt before.

It was never about how good they were, it was always about how bad your relationship got with yourself.

I will complete everything my soul has come to do on this earth, and I will not leave until it's accomplished. I'm not coming back here...I'm going back to the creator.

The question is…are you being a good person or are you being a weak person? Everyone uses the excuse that they are a "good" person, and that's the reason they continue to let people mistreat them. But the truth is, sometimes they have just forgotten their strength and self-worth. Is there any glory in being a "good" person to someone if they are constantly making you feel weak?

You're not crazy for feeling upset at someone. It doesn't make you a bad person for not forgiving them yet. You're not lazy because you're not motivated all the time. Things move and flow…it's a process.

The message of using your thoughts to create your life is seeming to get lost amongst all the noise. But let me assure you, it's still the highest truth.

Everyone has demons trying to make them to return to bad habits. Keep fighting them.

In the end, the way they treated you will haunt them more.

Sometimes I'm scared to be vulnerable. But then I remember that it's my vulnerability that can truly change the world. Sometimes there's so much pain. So lost, so confused, so unworthy...

Why are we all so scared to show our pain? It's the other half of life.

Sometimes I feel sad, sometimes I feel happy. Sometimes I feel angry, sometimes I feel at peace. Sometimes I feel lazy, sometimes I feel motivated. I'm human. And so are you...stop being so hard on yourself.

Connecting with the light and having inner peace is the only true way. That calmness is the only way to true confidence, true faith. Life is not worth living without it. You're not really alive, just existing. Be grounded like a tree trunk stuck firmly in the ground. Everything else will grow from there. Give this wisdom homage and respect every day. All else will fade away. All else will make sense.

Think about all the people who like you, or have liked you. I bet you've always been yourself. But whenever you've acted out of character to make someone like you, it's never worked. What does that tell you? The important lesson here isn't just "always be yourself", it's "be content in being with someone who you feel comfortable being yourself with".

Loving yourself cancels-out taking things personally.

Just remember, there's more to life than your phone.

The most successful relationships are those which both people subconsciously enter asking "What can I give this person?". When you enter in a selfish space of "What can this person offer me?" it will never work. And that's the problem with a lot of society today... it's all about US.

If you feel lost, it's because you worship the outside more than the inside.

Instead of always thinking 'I should be stronger than this, I should be acting different than this, I should be… etc," think "I will be stronger than this, I will be…etc." Things take time. Stop adding unnecessary pressure. Life has pages.

Just because you discover that someone's behaviour towards you has more to do with their problems than it does with yours, it doesn't mean you have to fix them. You can't fix everyone.

The way I have learnt to live life to the fullest is to constantly remind myself..."Every moment I am dying."

Men and women will always be a mystery to one another. Look how much we talk about each other and we have lived on this earth together for so long. Doesn't that say something? I don't believe we are ever meant to work it out...but that's what makes the pursuit so beautiful.

It's not really the rejection that hurts…it's that we know we gave more of ourselves than we should have. We were too invested emotionally and mentally too soon, even if the other person never knew how much they consumed us. It's an internal battle. And that's what hurts. We are disappointed in ourselves and think, "You still haven't learnt after all your experiences!"

What really hurts is not that we lost them, it's that we feel we gave away parts of ourselves. We feel that if we acted the way we normally do, it could have been a different outcome, even if just a difference in the way we now feel. And that's the hard part...thinking it could have been different if we were different. And people can keep saying, "Oh it just wasn't meant to be", and maybe they're right. But I do know one thing - unless we take accountability and say, "I don't want to be that insecure with anyone that soon again. I don't want to let someone I've just met determine my happinesss so much ever again," we won't make the proper pursuit to get off that wheel. There is liking someone, and then there is obsession. Obsession is never good for the soul.

I noticed that for a big part of last year, I was getting attached to people I didn't even really know or like. It was all due to a lack of direction in that moment and feeling like I lacked control of myself and my future.

Certain things serve a purpose in your life at different stages, however it is ok to turn the page. The way I know if something is no longer serving me, is by how much I regret it after I do it. I'm someone who needs to constantly learn the hard way in order to stop something...it's just the way I'm built. So if I have done something most of my life (for example drinking and partying) and it was never too much of a regret, than I know it was still serving me to learn to a degree. However when it gets to the point where my regret is far greater than the enjoyment I had when I was doing it, it's time to STOP.

We will know by the way something makes us feel if it has a place in our life anymore. If you stay focused on the feeling, you will make better decisions. The more you regret something and the excuses to keep doing it run out, let it be and turn the page. Greater things await on the other side.

Getting weak doesn't define you. Finding the strength to keep going through your weakness does. I'll tell you one thing….I'm far from perfect. I make so many mistakes. And I'm learning to be ok with that.

Have you ever noticed that you could be on top of the world one moment and then the slightest little thing happens, and you spiral out of control? You lose control of your mind and emotions rapidly? I believe this is because even though we think we are in a great place, we are actually on the edge.

I think in modern society we are living on the edge of insanity more than what we think. This has a lot to do with the constant sensory input we are receiving on a daily basis. We are constantly bombarded with insecurities on a screen, lights and sounds in a city environment, bombardment of technology. I don't think our brain has been able to adapt as quick as what we think to these constant high frequencies. They all continue to pile up, and eventually we fall off that edge. It's like we keep going in this false sense of security that everything is ok...but it's not. The answer...

We need nature. We need those low frequencies to balance our energies. I don't think future generations will need those low frequencies as much because they will adapt, but we are at the cusp of all of this. We still need it greatly. We need that stillness, that silence. Nature is a filtration system for our negative energy. Just like it absorbs carbon dioxide and gives oxygen, it also absorbs our negative energy and gives us positive energy.

They hate, but secretly revere the ones they don't have the courage to be.

When you're driving a car, if you stay focused on the rear view mirror, you're going to crash. It's far more important looking forward. Stop living in your past... you're not there anymore.

You know how you said that nothing really excites you anymore? Maybe you're just learning to be more content. I think we evolve and learn to just "be". And that is a beautiful thing. We don't always need...we have. And there's fulfilment in that energy if we accept it.

So often, people chase something they have already had, but gave up. Love and kindness are just two of those things.

I found where God lives…the heart. I know how God
feels…love.

All the pieces of the puzzle fit together to make the bigger picture you want for your life...if you believe it so.

If you're dating, you're not exempt from losing yourself to certain people. It's ignorant to think that just because it's happened to you before and you've "learnt your lesson", that it will never happen to you again. It can happen to anyone at any time, but there is a way to manage it...

You have to create distance from that person. When you start obsessing over someone to the point where you are waiting for every one of their texts or your happiness has become solely dependant on the attention they are giving you, you have to stop engaging in any contact. This might seem like an unhealthy way of dealing with it, but I disagree. What's the alternative? Keep going with that energy and dig a deeper hole for yourself? Let me ask you a question...When has starting with that energy ever worked-out? If you feel like it, you can politely tell them you are just taking time out for yourself at the moment.

You may engage in contact again after a while, but not until you have pulled yourself together. Then people will say "Oh but you aren't being yourself then, because that's how you felt at the time." My argument to that is...what part of yourself are you being? The one who is willing to bend and change to make someone like you? The one who is always feeling vulnerable, needy and powerless? You're better than that. Create distance, recollect yourself, and then you can engage again if you feel you're in a better place. If the person is "lost" in the meantime, you really haven't lost anything. You could lose a lot more...think of your past experiences when you've pursued something in that state.

The way someone treats you isn't a reflection of who you are, it's a reflection of who they are.

I've often heard many people play around with the idea that we have multiple life paths, and I think that comes from thinking we have multiple options to choose from in every moment. But I don't think we do. I think we have two paths...the one of our glory (evolution) and the one of our demise (lack of evolution).

I've thought deeply about the concept of opposites and the way it's also been described not just in philosophy but also in science throughout history. Positive and negative, sadness and happiness, the sun and the moon, yin and yang, etc etc. There is this fascination with polarity, the two sides. I think those visions we get of how great our life could be is one path and the other of doubt and despair is the other. That choice in every moment to choose what will serve that glory path or the path of demise are always available, always just as real. There is always a parallel universe but it's not something in the distance, it's always available to choose. One is just as real and set out like the other... you choose which path you walk in every moment.

So many times in my life I've felt stuck and like there was no where else to turn. But now looking back, there was always another way. And that's why I'm here right now.

There's always a way…be patient.

For a long time, I denied love. Not just distancing myself when I was offered it, but the very existence of it. I said that what I had felt in the past for people was only lust and delusion. Looking back, it's always easy to say things weren't as they seemed at that time. But I must truly admit, when I was there, it felt like love had completely consumed me. To look into their eyes, truly let go and whisper for the first time, "I love you." That moment...it felt like the most powerful force in Universe.

But then I have to admit, I still question...was it really "love"? What is truly loving someone? Does it require loving them for who they are as a person or how they treated me?

Usually the things that stress us the most are the things we want, not the things we need. If we can acknowledge this and realise that it's only the things that we need that truly make us content, then we will stress less in every day life. We should never let the pull towards what we want cloud the contentment of having what we need to breathe, feel love and survive.

People always ask me how I am able to be at peace more times than not. My answer… "I live more on the inside, than the outside."

Women have evolved so much, and fast. Through their open mind and constant practise of things like yoga, reading, meditation, Pilates, energy work, spirituality and learning new skills has helped them achieve things another generation would have once thought impossible. The way they band together for a common greatness is truly admirable. This might sound like I'm writing this for a reaction or to side with women. But I didn't…I wrote it in my bedroom when I was alone in deep thought and analysis. It is not just by opportunity they have achieved so much, it's by seizing those opportunities with everything they have.

I think as time passes, you will realise you never really loved them for who they were, and a lot was built on lust and delusion. A projection of what you hoped for. You couldn't really love someone for who they are if they don't respect you or aren't loyal till the end. At times it's our insecurities that just make us want them to love us. It's a lacking within self. I know this might be hard to digest or even comprehend, but in time you will realise this wasn't nearly as real as it seems right now. I think the best thing you can do is let them leave. We don't beg when we have done nothing wrong, when our intentions were pure. Put-up with all the emotions that you have to, but don't show them. When a person leaves, they do not deserve anything more from us.

Being "awakened" is to understand that your thoughts create most of your life. Being "enlightened" is leading that life with love.

Nelson Mandela was 45 when he got sentenced to prison. He got out when he was 72 and a year later became president of South Africa. Then he passed away 23 years after that at 95. We have a long life. He was in jail for 27 years! Just think about that for a moment. So, savour the moments and live in the present. We have a lot of time to do what we want. Breathe…you've got this.

I've had times when I've felt like I was drowning. I couldn't breath, I couldn't see. But somehow, I always kept one finger above the water...and just when I thought I was going to give up, something always came along and pulled me out. You must hold on, even just a little. Something is going to change.

When you don't want to be anyone else but yourself, you've made it to the highest level of being.

The best way to make peace with the past is by visualising the future. All else happens in the present.

The 4th and 7th Chakra's are starting to open/sync again after 6 months of suppression. Pressure has been building. The next cosmic creative wave is coming… and it's going to be bigger than I could have ever imagined. I can feel it. Immortality awaits. I will be guided, I always have been. I didn't choose this. It chose me.

I always sugar coat when I explain what happened to me when I was 23… when I was thrown down the rabbit hole. I don't really know how to explain it, that's the truth. My words are finite, what happened to me wasn't. It was magnificent, scary, magical, consuming, it completely stripped me bear and made me one with everything. I didn't read any books or watch anything to go through it. I didn't learn it. I had no idea what was happening to me, it just was. And what I found, no one can take away from me…ever. I found the Source. And it's still only beginning to unfold to the outside realm. That's why when people ask me, "What are you? Are you spiritual?" I will never use such terms. To say that I am "Spiritual" which insinuates that I am different to something else, proves that I haven't really gone 'through it.' When you have really gone 'through it', you do not label it, or yourself. My answer always is… "I am who I am, and that is everything."

You see, the difference is...I'm not afraid to walk through hell and conquer my demons.

Sometimes you go through life manifesting and in your flow, and then an experience happens and you feel that channel is blocked. But don't be too anxious about it. It just means you need to be patient as it unblocks. Because when it does, that channel widens and you tap into more of your manifestation power. Your connection with the source gets wider and deeper. So if you're in that stage where you feel energetic blocks within you, just know that it will pass, you will open, and greater feelings are coming.

I used to hold grudges against those who hurt me. In some weird way I wanted them to feel the pain they had caused me, whether for my own selfish satisfaction or for them to learn. But I realised that's not the space that serves me, this world, or them. Love...that's the answer. Wish them love. We all need more of that.

Sometimes you never got to say what you wanted to someone and it's not because you were weak, it's because you knew deep down they weren't ready to hear it. They didn't want to hear it. So you paused, thought about it, and let them walk off thinking they did nothing wrong. And that's ok...their weakness was shown by their loose mouth. Their lack of evolution was shown by their unwillingness to listen. Their shortage of growth from not being willing to learn about oneself. Be proud, you had control. And in the end, they will have to find out the hard way. The Universe is merciless in what it does to humble people.

When people ask me "Who are you?" I answer, "I am who I am at any given moment."

If your intentions were pure, don't let them make you question who you are.

All the pain you've gone through, all the times you've walked through hell in your mind, all the times you've fallen. None of it has been in vein. A new version of you is coming. God has blessings coming for you… be open to them. Stay true to who you are, you are amazing. Don't let them make you think otherwise.

Self-sabotage is real. People can't believe they have found a good thing because they are not yet secure within themselves. They will constantly look for cracks, and if they can't find big enough ones, they will get a sledgehammer and hit those cracks so hard they end up falling through.

She had a chip on her shoulder…that's why she seemed imbalanced.

When they have a high level of self-entitlement in regards to what they think they are, rather than who they are, you will feel it early on. Run! It will feel transactional. This will lead them to be constantly belittling, controlling, condescending, nit picky and aggravated often. They won't let you be yourself. Rarely wrong, a level of grandiosity. But just know this is their insecurities on a very deep level.

If they made you feel like they were looking for something real, but then you realised that their willingness to connect was conditional on external things, it's better they are gone. Only a person with extreme low self esteem seeks relationships like that. And the saddest thing is, sometimes they don't even see it.

I was the artist... she was the con-artist.

Your eyes are at the mercy of how you feel about yourself. What you feel on the inside is what you will see on the outside.

To master self is not to try and hold onto happiness…
it's to hold onto nothing.

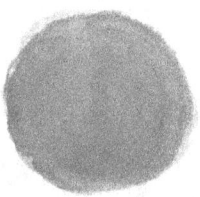

I had to sit down today. It hit me...God showed me what's coming. It was overwhelming. And all I heard was a deep voice inside say, "Get ready." They say it's ego, but they only hate what they don't understand. God's plan has no ego...it's just truth, it's just love.

When you're obsessing over someone, it's never a reflection of how good they are, but always a reflection of how bad your relationship has become with yourself. When you are truly in a space of self-love, no one can ever have that much power over you. So instead of putting your focus on why they aren't giving you attention, put it towards asking yourself why you're not giving yourself enough.

When you're an empath, you always try to find the good in people and remember the acts of kindness they did, even if they were few. You ignore all the rest and only look at the best and try to hold onto that. But just remember, that is not the truth...nowhere close to it. Your real experience was something very different. Don't ignore that.

If you have completed writing in every page,
please feel free to fill in the next page....

THOUGHTS AND FEELINGS

VOLUME ONE

Co-written by

Daniel Chidiac   &   _____

For posting on social media and for us to re-share, please tag

 @danielchidiac

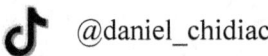 @daniel_chidiac

and use the hashtag #ThoughtsAndFeelings

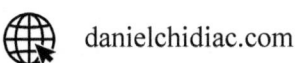 danielchidiac.com